WHAT'S YOUR VIEW?

THE IMPACT OF BIG BUSINESS

Melanie Jarman

FRANKLIN WATTS
LONDON • SYDNEY

First published in 2006 by
Franklin Watts
338 Euston Road
London NW1 3BH

Franklin Watts Australia
Hachette Children's Books
Level 17/207 Kent Street
Sydney NSW 2000

© Franklin Watts 2006

ISBN 0 7496 6311 1
Dewey Classification: 338.7

Series editor: Sarah Peutrill
Art director: Jonathan Hair
Design: Proof Books
Picture researcher: Sophie Hartley

Picture and text credits: see page 48.
Every attempt has been made to clear
copyright. Should there be any inadvertent
omission please apply to the publisher for
rectification.

Note on websites:
Every effort has been made by the Publishers
to ensure that the websites in this book
contain no inappropriate or offensive
material. However, because of the nature of
the Internet, it is impossible to guarantee
that the contents of these sites will not be
altered. We strongly advise that Internet
access is supervised by a responsible adult.

A CIP catalogue record for this book is
available from the British Library.

Contents

What's the issue?

Big businesses play a role in almost every part of our lives. They produce the clothes that many of us wear and the food that many of us eat. They distribute the water that runs from our taps and the electricity that powers our machines. They produce most of the TV programmes, newspapers and magazines that shape the way in which we view the world.

Multinationals

Many big businesses have huge incomes that can be the size of the economies of small countries. Operating across national borders and with huge resources at their disposal, these multinationals are possibly the most powerful institutions in the world.

Making an impact

This book examines the impact of big businesses on the world. While they produce material goods and offer a range of services, their operations have also been said to lead to environmental problems, poor working conditions and political corruption.

Profit motive

What drives these powerful institutions? Corporate law says that the task big business must put above all others is that of making money for their shareholders. Their ultimate legal responsibility is to make a profit, and their decision-making will be influenced by whether or not the outcome generates money. This means that it is important to move beyond

moral judgements of whether the impact of big business is simply 'good' or 'bad': questions around how laws relevant to big businesses are made, interpreted and implemented are also important.

Society's interest?

At the heart of the debate on the impact of big business lies the question of what is in the best interest of society. With significant resources at their disposal, big businesses have the capacity to shape the way in which the world works. Are they always in the best position to do so? Given that their main responsibility is to make a profit, are there areas from which big business should be excluded, for example water distribution, policing society, or providing health services? Or are big businesses the only institutions that have the resources to provide services efficiently? Even if we wanted to limit the activity and impact of big business, would this be possible, given the extent of their power and influence?

With the presence of big businesses in all of our lives, each of us will have direct experience of, and important views on, the impact that they make.

Note on quotes

Quotes presented in this book in a specific context should not be understood to commit their source to one side of that debate. They are simply illustrations of the possible viewpoints in each debate.

Big business forms the backdrop to our lives in a range of ways. Here, two women have lunch in the shadow of an Olympics advertisement sponsored by the fast-food giant McDonalds.

Q: Does big business rule the world?

THE SIZE of big businesses makes them extremely powerful. Some of them have more money than the countries in which they operate. Many governments make laws to dictate the ways businesses work, for instance to protect the health and safety of employees. However, because of their financial power, businesses are able to influence governments and some people say that they have gone too far in using this influence.

YES

'American business and the organisations that represent them are more active and needed in Washington than ever before. The economic stakes are too high – and the issues too complex – to leave the decision to others.'

John J Castellani,
Business Roundtable President

'Corporations have enormous lobbying power over governments, control much of the media, exploit the law to their own advantage (they can and do afford all the best lawyers) and use that power to maintain and extend their dominance.'

Rebecca Spencer, Corporate Watch UK

NO

'If the government is not able to maintain a favourable business climate, businesses may have the power to "bail out" from the economy and invest elsewhere since less industrialised nations are presently competing for foreign investments. However ... business is dependent on the government as much as the government is dependent on business.'

Johan Olsson, MBA graduate,
Griffith University, Australia

'The government sets the rules. They provide the structure within which we do business.'

Hank McKinnell, Chair of Business Roundtable and Chair and CEO of Pfizer Inc

✪ STATISTICALLY SPEAKING

• Over 70% of lobbyists at the European Parliament in Brussels work for big businesses, while only 20% represent non-governmental organisations (NGOs) such as trade unions, public health organisations and environmental groups.

• In the US, more than three-quarters of the 205 Cabinet secretaries appointed between 1897 and 1972 were directors of corporations or came from corporate law firms.

EGYPT

ECUADOR

CASE STUDY

BIG BUSINESS AND THE WORLD TRADE ORGANISATION

The World Trade Organisation (WTO) sets rules for international trade. These cover food and environmental standards, farming, patent law and more. Though it is unelected, the WTO has the power to challenge countries' policies if it thinks they are barriers to international trade. Government trade representatives often ask big businesses for their views on international trading rules. But sometimes big businesses may have too much influence. For example, minutes of the private meetings of a trade committee in 1999 and 2001 showed that government officials leaked secret documents to business leaders, as well as inside information on the negotiating positions of the European community, the US and developing nations.

Delegates at a meeting of the World Trade Organisation study papers at the WTO's headquarters in Geneva. Approximately 150 countries are members of the WTO but decision-making tends to be dominated by the wealthier nations.

Large companies by revenue, millions US$

Company	Country of Origin	2001 revenue	Compared to country economies
Wal-Mart	US	219,812	(approx. size Sweden)
ExxonMobil	US	191,581	(larger than Turkey)
General Motors	US	177,260	(larger than Denmark)
Ford Motor	US	162,412	(larger than Poland)
DaimlerChrysler	Germany	149,608	(larger than Norway)

MORE TO THINK ABOUT

Is it wrong for big business to rule the world? Why? If business shouldn't rule the world, then who should?

FIND OUT MORE: www.oneworld.net www.wto.org www.wdm.org.uk

Q: Are the people who run big businesses paid too much?

STAFF AT the top of big businesses are usually paid very well – some would argue too well. Often high levels of pay are maintained even when a business appears to be failing. Some say that this is fair because these people work long hours and carry a lot of responsibility. Others suggest that this applies to staff at all levels in a company, as well as to people such as teachers, and wages should be distributed in a fairer way.

NO

'At the end of the day, we have to retain and attract top people. In terms of [pay], we have to recognise we are increasingly operating in a global market place.'
Keith Ince, Portfolio Partners

✗ 'In a world where C-list non-entity Kerry McFadden is due to earn £2 million plus from winning "I'm a Celebrity" [reality TV programme] ... how much would you pay a boss of a company that was successful – as [GlaxoSmithKline] hopes to be – in ridding the world of malaria?'
Management Today

✗ 'As much as people gripe about City boys and girls [people who work in well-paid financial jobs], they too could join ... if they were prepared to work long hours in a macho culture at a job that manages to be simultaneously stressful and boring. So most City jobs, while very well paid, are not necessarily overpaid.'
Rhymer Rigby, Management Today

Sir Christopher Gent, chief executive of mobile phone company Vodafone, retired on an annual pension of about £662,000.

YES

'It bothers me sometimes when you see the rewards these guys are giving themselves ... I suspect they would work just as hard if they were on a tenth of what they earn. People who want to achieve will achieve, regardless of money.'

Jan Luthman, fund manager

'Excessive CEO pay takes dollars out of the pockets of shareholders – including the retirement savings of America's working families.'

American Federation of Labour and Congress of Industrial Organisations

'The executives claim that they are paid no more than they have earned, but in truth they have simply manoeuvred themselves into positions in which they can extract fantastic rewards, even when they are sacked for poor performance ... In the United States, golden goodbyes [a large sum given to a director on retirement] have given way to 'platinum parachutes': dismissal payments of $100 million or more.'

George Monbiot, writer and campaigner

� STATISTICALLY SPEAKING

• Between 1970 and 2001, average pay among the top 100 executives rose from 35 times that of the average worker to more than 500 times as much.

CONFLICTING EVIDENCE?

According to research, FTSE 100 boardroom salaries were set to rise just 5% in 2005.

Salary is just one part of a chief executive's pay package. They are likely to also receive bonuses, which can be up to 100% of salary and the pay-out rate for these is 72%. At the end of Sir Christopher Gent's days at Vodafone, company executives' basic salaries accounted for about a fifth of their potential pay packages, with the rest made up of performance-related bonuses, shares and options [the right to buy or sell shares in a business].

✖ STATISTICALLY SPEAKING

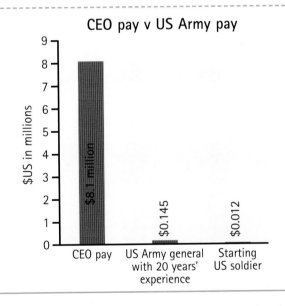

CEO pay v US Army pay

$US in millions

- CEO pay — $8.1 million
- US Army general with 20 years' experience — $0.145
- Starting US soldier — $0.012

MORE TO THINK ABOUT

This issue raises other questions: How much money does anyone need? Should there be a maximum wage limit, in the way that some countries have a minimum wage limit?

FIND OUT MORE: www.corporatepolicy.org   www.clickmt.com

Q: Do shareholders have real power?

THE MAIN responsibility of a big business is to make money for its investors – the shareholders. If large numbers of shareholders were unhappy with company behaviour they could withdraw their investments, forcing a company to re-think or to collapse. However this rarely happens. In practice, the large number of shares issued by companies makes it difficult for small shareholders to influence policy. Shareholders come together once a year at a company's annual general meeting (AGM).

YES

'The outcome of the [shareholder] vote means that the principles of good practice have been upheld. In particular it shows that shareholders will not tolerate arrangements that have potential to reward executives for failure.'

Peter Montagon, Association of British Insurers, after more than half of GlaxoSmithKline shareholders voted against an executive pay package

'Imagine what would happen on the stock markets of the world if a majority of small shareholders in a [corporation which did business with a regime that was denying basic human rights to its peoples] agreed to sell their stock on the same day ... It would certainly focus the minds of their chief executives on deciding whether such business was worth a financial crisis for their organisation.'

Website Shareholder Power

Shareholders queue up for an annual general meeting of a large retail company.

✣ STATISTICALLY SPEAKING

• From 2000–2003 nearly half of all shareholder resolutions to 81 large US corporations were related to Corporate Social Responsibility (CSR), where a business considers how its activities impact on social and environmental issues.

The number of Corporate Social Responsibility proposals per year in five categories for four different years

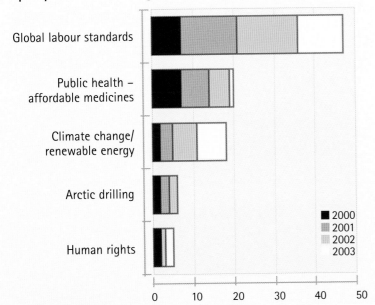

'We are the risk takers, you are the money takers ... I see you sitting up there in your first class compartment ... with pensions that people would die for ... and we sit in the third class compartment on wooden seats, feeling every bump.'

Comment from shareholder Ken Colvert at a mobile phone company AGM

'Shareholder resolutions [though useful for drawing public attention to corporate misdeeds are not] in any way, a substitute for effective government regulation.'

Simon Billenness, Trillium Asset Management

CASE STUDY

ETHICS FOR USS CAMPAIGN

The Universities Superannuation Scheme (USS) is a £19 billion pension fund for university staff in the UK. A group of USS members have organised campaigns to raise concerns over how their pensions are invested. They have convinced managers of the pension fund to consider ethical issues in their investment choices. This has led to:

• new investment guidelines
• successful lobbying of GlaxoSmithKline to lower the price of its anti-AIDS drugs in South Africa
• USS votes on resolutions at company annual general meetings to send messages of disapproval to companies where necessary. These are often in regard to environmental policy.

MORE TO THINK ABOUT

Many shares are not held by individuals, but by pension funds and insurance companies: their shareholders would have to influence them before they attempted to exercise their power as shareholders in any other organisation.

Q: Do corporations behave responsibly?

A FAMOUS economist called Milton Friedman once declared that it is irresponsible for a business to think about its social or environmental impact, as its most important responsibility is to make a profit. Friedman was referring to a business's legal obligation to make money for its shareholders. Many people argue, however, that big businesses should consider their impacts in the communities in which they work and on the environment in which they operate.

YES 'The International Chamber of Commerce has become a highly valued partner of the United Nations. Together, we promote free and fair trade as one of the best ways for countries to overcome poverty.'
Kofi Annan, Secretary-General of the United Nations

'The Coca-Cola Company and its local bottling partners do a lot more than simply produce delicious beverages. We help build schools, provide job training in developing communities, and partner with civic organisations to help people bring their dreams to life.'
Coca-Cola Company website

'After having a baby, I was able to work all kinds of shifts due to Wal-Mart's flexible schedules ... Wal-Mart allows me to be a working mum and a good mum at the same time.'
Tiffany, Pharmacy Division, Wal-Mart

Celebrations at the opening of a Wal-Mart store in Texas in 2004. Relations between the company and its employees have not always been good. (See 'Caught in the act', opposite).

- 80% of companies in the FTSE 100 now issue reports on corporate social responsibility.
- 86% of investors believe that social and environmental risk-management improves a company's market value in the long term.

Caught in the act:

Company	Offence	Fine/settlement
Bayer	Deliberately overcharging the US Medicaid insurance programme	US$250 million (2003)
Boeing	Bribery, fraud, kickbacks, military contract and export law violations	US$100 million (1999–2001)
Coca-Cola	Settlement of a race-discrimination suit by black employees	US$192.5 million (2001)
Wal-Mart	World's largest retailer caught forcing employees to work unpaid overtime	US$50 million (2000)

CASE STUDY

BAT

All British American Tobacco (BAT) farmers in Kenya have a contract for their work. Under the heading 'Environmental and Safety Issues for Farmers' the contract says that farmers should 'always wear boots, gloves and clothes that cover the whole body'.

Three brothers employed by BAT Kenya have talked of their experience of the time that the company gave them the boots and overalls: 'They said the cost would be deducted from our [wages] ... When we protested they said they had paid for the boots and for the tailors to make the overalls and therefore we had to pay them'.

NO 'The international community has not awakened fully to the grim nature of this highly sophisticated if unconventional war being waged by very powerful multinationals against a defenceless people and their environment.'

Ken Saro Wiwa, speaking about the situation in the Niger Delta (Wiwa was later hanged by the Nigerian military government after a trial that was criticised by human rights organisations)

✖ 'The corporation is a dictatorship ... run as a centrally-planned economy with an extensive bureaucracy. Workers within the system have few rights, they are increasingly under tight surveillance, and the penalty for disobedience is loss of livelihood.'

Rebecca Spencer, Corporate Watch UK

✖ 'There is always somebody who pays, and international business is generally the main source of corruption.'

George Soros, international financier

MORE TO THINK ABOUT

Considering a company's effect on the wider world, Corporate Social Responsibility (CSR) is seen as an important tool by businesses that are concerned about their public image. However, to ensure that CSR is about more than marketing, questions need to be asked: is it used as a mask for destructive behaviour? Does it distract from effective regulation of businesses?

Q: Should big business be subject to international laws?

WHEN BUSINESSES operate in many countries (some of which may have weak legal systems or may be very keen to attract investment) it can be difficult to regulate their behaviour. Businesses themselves have tried to address this by drawing up voluntary codes of conduct. But these codes of conduct are often policed by the businesses to which they apply, and some people argue that enforced laws are necessary to protect people and the environment.

YES 'We have to make businesses consider the impacts of their products on society and the environment – and not wait for governments to regulate for every single eventuality separately, where a product causes harm, or worse: just let consumers do the complicated work of holding companies in check for their ethical performance.'

Deborah Doane, Chair, CORE Coalition

'Union Carbide Corporation was responsible for a [long list] of failures in the period leading up to the gas leak. Bhopal shows how readily some companies can evade their human rights responsibilities. There is a real need for global human rights standards for corporations.'

Benedict Southworth, Amnesty International

CASE STUDY 1

BHOPAL

In 1984, a Union Carbide Corporation plant in Bhopal, India leaked deadly gas. Up to 20,000 people died as a result of the accident and more than 120,000 still suffer from related illnesses. The Dow Chemical Company bought Union Carbide in 2001 but has refused to clean up the site or provide compensation.

This woman and many others were blinded by the Bhopal chemical leak.

NO 'Imposing new legal requirements will add to company costs – likely to fall especially heavily on small and medium-sized enterprises without necessarily raising environmental or social standards. Unlike financial accounting criteria, environmental and labour protection issues do not apply with equal relevance to all companies.'

Confederation of British Industry

X 'I believe that self-regulation encourages businesses to develop principles about the way they behave that go much deeper into the business process than they do when a business is simply asked to show that it is meeting specific requirements required by a rule or a law. There is a danger inherent in forcing companies to play by a fixed set of rules. Some will look for loopholes and ways to meet their requirements without doing more than the bare minimum.'

Morris Tabaksblat, Chairman of publishers Reed Elsevier and winner of FIRST magazine's award for responsible capitalism

✿ STATISTICALLY SPEAKING

• Over 639 organisations voluntarily use the Sustainability Reporting Guidelines. These are for voluntary use by organisations for reporting on the economic, environmental and social aspects of their activities.

CASE STUDY 2

CAPE PLC AND ASBESTOSIS

In 2003 the High Court in the UK approved a compensation settlement of £7.5 million for the 7,500 South African miners who had been exposed to asbestos by UK company, Cape plc. Before a trial could even begin, Cape spent three years arguing that the case should be moved to the South African courts.

Cecil Skeffers of community group Concerned People Against Asbestos (CPAA) said: 'While we can't forget the effects Cape's operations have had on thousands of people, we are delighted that Cape have finally made a settlement. We hope this will be an example to other multinational companies who practise in similar ways.'

Richard Meeran, a lawyer who worked on the case said: 'Multinationals now recognise that if they apply double standards and fail to protect workers and the environment, they are likely to be held legally accountable.'

MORE TO THINK ABOUT

Even if companies have to comply with international laws, businesses may treat a fine as an additional cost of doing business. However, international laws for big businesses may have a knock-on effect on the countries in which they operate: the threat of breaking human rights laws may put businesses off investing in countries with repressive governments.

Q: Are oil companies too powerful?

OIL IS a crucial part of many people's lives. It is used in heating and transport. It is used to make plastics and to make fertilisers for crops. Because oil is so important, the businesses that are involved in the oil industry are very powerful. Some say they have become too powerful and have too great a say in world affairs.

YES

'Whoever owns [Romania's main oil company] has an important word to say in the economy, and whoever has an important word to say in the economy also has an important word to say in politics.'

Adrian Nastase,
Romanian Prime Minister

'The [Baku-Ceyhan pipeline] project is governed by [agreements with Azerbaijan, Kazakhstan, Georgia and Turkey] which ... allow BP to demand compensation from the governments should any law (including environmental, social or human rights law) make the pipeline less profitable.'

Baku-Ceyhan Campaign

'Many universities, operating in a climate of ever-tighter public funding, are only too eager to please big business. In return for corporate sponsorship and contracts, universities are encouraging oil companies to steer the research agenda, tailoring courses to meet corporate personnel demands and awarding high profile positions to oil executives.'

Andrew Simms, New Economics Foundation

BP's Baku-Ceyhan pipeline carries oil for approximately 1,700 km for export to western markets. The opening ceremony was attended by the US energy secretary alongside the presidents of Azerbaijan, Georgia, Turkey and Kazakhstan.

NO 'OPEC does not control the oil market ... However, OPEC's oil exports represent about 55% of the oil traded internationally. Therefore, OPEC can have a strong influence on the oil market, especially if it decides to reduce or increase its level of production.'
Organisation of Petroleum Exporting Countries (OPEC)

✗ 'The [oil] companies may not care about Amazon Indians, but they pay very close attention to the desires of their investors and shareholders.'
Matthew Yeomans,
'Oil: Anatomy of an Industry'

✗ 'External influences control how a project is designed and completed. The world around you has different perceptions of risk and communities will, in one way or another, force you to listen to them and to come to solutions which meet their needs as well as yours.'
Lord Browne, Group Chief Executive BP

CASE STUDY

OIL IN THE WHITE HOUSE

Some commentators are concerned that US President George W Bush comes under too much influence from oil companies. Oil companies were some of the biggest donors to his election campaigns and his cabinet includes strong links with the industry.

US Vice President Dick Cheney is a former Chair and Chief Executive of Halliburton Corporation, the world's biggest oil-services company. While he worked there he was important in negotiating a Caspian Sea pipeline for Chevron (now ChevronTexaco), whose board Secretary of State Condoleezza Rice sat on for 10 years. Rice had an oil tanker named after her when she left Chevron.

✺ STATISTICALLY SPEAKING

• Of the top 25 energy industry donors to the Republican Party (USA) before the November 2000 election, 18 had meetings with the energy task force that drew up the new administration's energy policy.

• The global oil industry is worth an estimated US$5 trillion annually. The three biggest oil companies, ExxonMobil, BP and Shell, are the world's second, third and fourth largest companies respectively.

2003 turnover in billions of US$

ExxonMobil (Esso)	237
BP	236
Shell	201

MORE TO THINK ABOUT

Climate change and a decreasing amount of accessible oil mean that energy sources will begin to change. Will oil companies be able to maintain their control over energy sources? Will the insurance industry become more powerful by demanding a move away from oil, as damage resulting from climate change increases?

FIND OUT MORE: www.amazonwatch.org www.opec.org
www.bpamoco.org.uk

Q: Do banks make too much profit?

BANKS CAN be very profitable businesses. When banks make loans they charge a fee called interest, so the more loans that their customers take out on their credit cards, or to buy houses, the more money the bank makes. They also make money by charging customers for late payments or for special services.

Calling itself 'the world's local bank', HSBC is one of the largest banking groups in the world. It has an international network of over 9,800 offices in 77 countries.

YES

'Most of the UK banks make a profit by closing branches and sacking staff, not by being efficient or providing or improving services. Unfortunately, I suspect that the banks are all as bad as one another and, as we all have to bank somewhere, they have become hugely complacent.'

Tony Hague, UK,
BBC Online Talking Point

'Foreign banks – Citibank, Chase Manhattan Bank, Bank of America, Credit Suisse and Lloyds Bank ... having bled the nation of capital, lent Argentina back its own money at rates that can only be called usury.'

Greg Palast, journalist, 2002

CASE STUDY

GRAMEEN BANK, BANGLADESH

More than half the population of the world cannot use conventional banks, which are based on the principle that the more you have, the more you can get. For example, to open a bank account or to get a loan people may have to prove that they already have some assets.

But not all banks are solely motivated by profit. The Grameen Bank aims to make resources available for poor people to get out of poverty. It does not ask people to prove that they already have assets but is based on a system of trust and accountability.

Managing Director Professor Muhammad Yunus suggests that if banks' services can be made available to people on terms that suit them then 'these millions of small people with their millions of small pursuits can add up to create the biggest development wonder'.

NO 'Dissatisfaction with the banks is omnipresent and will probably remain thus. We complain about our treatment as customers but overwhelmingly we do not exercise the one meaningful remedy available to us in a competitive marketplace: that is, we do not shop around for a better deal.'

Sydney Morning Herald, Australia

✗ 'What is wrong with the banks making a profit? What is wrong with anyone making a profit? It's their business, and banking has become as easy as it is now precisely because they had been making profits. Let them do their business, it is ultimately to our benefit.'

Horia Paraschivescu, Romania, BBC Online Talking Point

Banks have to operate services such as cash machines.

✱ STATISTICALLY SPEAKING

• Approximately US$1,200 billion worth of currency is traded daily on the foreign exchange market. Advances in technology have weakened banks' control of this market, although the cost of trading technology means that the bigger banks still dominate.

• On a global level, there is US$100 trillion of debt outstanding, but only US$33 trillion of income with which to repay that debt.

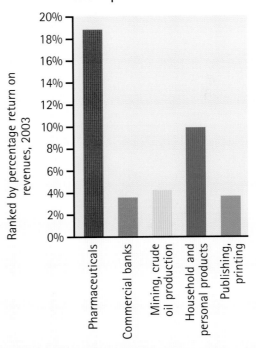

Most profitable industries

Ranked by percentage return on revenues, 2003

- Pharmaceuticals — ~19%
- Commercial banks — ~3.5%
- Mining, crude oil production — ~4.3%
- Household and personal products — ~10%
- Publishing, printing — ~3.8%

MORE TO THINK ABOUT

Will increased use of Internet banking have an impact on the profits of high street banks? What alternatives could people use to save or to borrow money?

Q: Have sports become just more big businesses?

SPORTS HAVE increasingly become about more than exercise or competition. There is a lot of money in sport – in sponsorship deals with companies that pay for equipment and training and from the media. Has this money become too important?

The International Olympic Committee resisted bids from pay-TV and chose to have the 2004 Games broadcast on free TV.

NO 'There were tremendous pressures on the IOC [International Olympic Committee] to sell out to the highest bidder for TV rights ... But to do that would have limited opportunities for people to see the Games.'

Michael Payne, the International Olympic Committee's Director of Global Broadcasting

✗ 'I'd be lying if I told you I didn't think about what I could make in free agency after this season. I still think about it. But I love being on this team. I wanted to stay. And I'm happy I'm staying.'

Tedy Brushci, US football player

YES

'Once known as the "gentleman's game", cricket today is fast becoming almost a mean gladiatorial sport ... Rules of field placements, no balls, penalty points have changed ... Commerce is the focal point of all these changes and commercialisation has according to me changed the very character of the game.'

Ashish S Chavan, lawyer

✓ 'Vodafone's £9m a year to sponsor [Manchester United] is worth it just in terms of cost per media impression alone.'

Tim Crow, sponsorship consultancy director

✓ 'Sport in the [Middle East] is currently enjoying a very high profile, as governments actively push participation and many states bid to host major sporting events to help them attract cash, rich tourists and corporations to the region.'

Sportbusiness.com

CASE STUDY

SPORTS STARS AS BRANDS

Sponsorship is the biggest of big business's relationships with sport. At the peak of his fame, English footballer David Beckham had sponsorship deals with at least six big businesses including Vodafone and Pepsi.

But sports stars themselves can also become a brand: over one million David Beckham shirts have been sold since he joined football team Real Madrid – over 50% of the club's shirt sales. Some have suggested that Beckham was signed not so much for his on-the-field skill, but for his ability to attract fans (and their money).

✳ STATISTICALLY SPEAKING

• The top-paid female athlete during 2003–2004 was Serena Williams, who earned $9.5 million. The top-paid men were Tiger Woods and Michael Schumacher, who earned $80 million each.

• 40% of the $1.1 billion that the top 50 highest earning sportspeople received in 2003 came from endorsements for products.

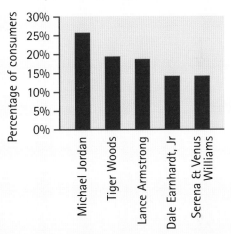

Proportion of consumers who will be 'much' or 'somewhat' more likely to buy a product based on a particular sports celebrity endorsement

MORE TO THINK ABOUT

Lower league teams may find that they cannot afford to buy better players or may have to sell their good players to generate income. However, the weaker the team the less likely they are to attract audiences or to win matches, leaving them in a difficult position. How do huge sums of sponsorship money going into a sport affect this?

Q: Do supermarkets offer choice and value?

SUPERMARKETS HAVE a central role in many peoples' lives. Most people in developed countries buy their food at supermarkets. Many of the food crops grown in developing countries are sold in supermarkets overseas. Supermarkets display a wide range of products, often at discount prices, and appear to offer a wide choice and better value than local shops. However, only a handful of food companies may be behind the many products on the shelves. Some people say that supermarkets abuse the power that comes from their size and importance in retail markets. This power will increase as supermarkets are now moving into selling clothes, medicines and financial services.

✪ STATISTICALLY SPEAKING

- Fifty years ago, farmers in Europe and North America received 45–60% of the money that consumers spent on food. Today, they receive 7% in the UK, 3.5% in the USA, and 18% in France.
- In 2002 the top 30 grocer retailers accounted for about 33% of global sales.

NO

'We use more pesticides than we'd like to, to try to meet the cosmetic standards set. Anything that reduces the appearance will increase the proportion rejected. Even so, a typical [rejection] might be 35% of what we send. If the supermarkets can't sell them, we don't get paid.'

Anonymous carrot grower (suppliers will often not comment publicly in case they get taken off the approved supplier list)

✖ 'Cheap food is a myth. The consumer really pays three times: once in the shop, a second time in taxes through direct subsidies to farmers, and finally indirectly in taxes cleaning up the mess left by industrial agriculture and subsidising the transport infrastructure.'

Lucy Michaels, Corporate Watch

✖ 'The opening of these big retailers has had a serious impact on local [retailers].'

Kosol Somchinda, President of Nakhon Ratchsima Chamber of Commerce, Thailand

✖ '[Here] in the USA ... a handful of corporations control everything. I try to shop at small stores for everything, but it is becoming harder to do so.'

Bryan, USA

Psychologists and food marketing experts are involved in planning the layout of supermarkets. Some food companies actually pay to have their goods displayed in a particular place in the store in the hope that this will bring them higher sales.

CASE STUDY 1

WAL-MART

A 2004 report by US Congressman George Miller found that the supermarket giant Wal-Mart was costing US taxpayers hundreds of millions of dollars a year in housing, medical and childcare needs, as the company failed to provide proper cover and wages for its employees. The Congressman also found that Wal-Mart was exploiting employees overseas, with workers in countries like China, Bangladesh and Honduras suffering because of the demands the company made on suppliers. One factory worker reported working 19-hour days for stretches of 10–15 days to meet Wal-Mart's price demands.

Q: Do supermarkets offer choice and value?

TESCO SUPERMARKETS

Tesco is the world's number three retailer, with over 2,300 stores across Europe and Asia. It has 326,000 staff and 12 million people shop at Tesco. Chief Executive Sir Terry Leahy says that the fact that people keep coming through the door means that Tesco must be doing something right. Director of Communications Lucy Neville-Rolfe describes the company's global reach as: 'We are international but we are local in national markets.'

CONFLICTING EVIDENCE?

'Food retailers will continue to work with their partners in the food chain to build a sustainable British dairy industry from which they are able to source supplies of the highest quality. We want to see an increased availability of British milk and increased innovation in the sector.'

Source: British Retail Consortium

Where the money goes for one litre of milk:

Farmers' cost to produce: 20p
Price paid to farmer: 17–18p
Supermarket shelf price: 43–45p

Source: Observer newspaper, 2004

YES 'Supermarkets make us richer. They are hugely efficient, forcing down costs ... They enrich our choice too. The shelves groan with fruit and vegetables that were unknown 40 years ago – or unknown in the winter, when they were out of season. Sure, they might be bad for inefficient grocers in their area. But they bring in huge footfall which actually helps other retailers. A new supermarket can actually revive a dead area of town ... The Work Foundation praised them for the number of jobs they create and the flexibility of the working patterns they offer – one reason why they are huge employers of women with family commitments and the over-50s.'

Dr Eamonn Butler,
blog on the Adam Smith Institute Website

Shoppers watch television screens while queuing to pay.

'In the 1950s, households were spending a third of their income on food, whilst now we spend less than a sixth of our income on groceries. Food items that were once [only available to] the well-off are now available to all.'

Fiona Moriarty, Director of the Scottish Retail Consortium

'A champion could be about to arrive, [which will bring] a better life for all.'

Daily Mail, on Wal-Mart's arrival in the UK

'One of the few drawbacks of living in New York City is the lack of true supermarkets (we have overgrown convenience stores that call themselves "supermarkets", but they're not even close). Whenever I visit friends or family in other cities and we go to a real supermarket ... well, it can make a grown New Yorker weep.'

Anon, USA

❈ STATISTICALLY SPEAKING

Exporting apples from South Africa to UK supermarkets

Each element in the supply chain adds to the retail price for apples to cover costs and margins.

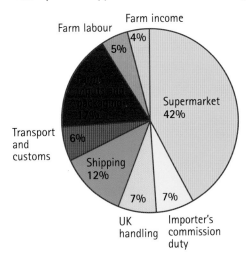

- Farm income 4%
- Farm labour 5%
- Farm inputs and packaging 17%
- Supermarket 42%
- Transport and customs 6%
- Shipping 12%
- UK handling 7%
- Importer's commission duty 7%

Source: 2003 data based on information from Deciduous Fruit Producers Trust and various exporters and importers

MORE TO THINK ABOUT

Most food for supermarkets travels a long way (even when it may be possible to grow the same product locally). This is known as 'food miles'. It often has an environmental cost in, for example, emissions from the planes transporting the food.

Q: Does the arms trade have benefits for anyone?

ONE OF the biggest businesses in the world is the trade in weapons. Arms companies claim that they contribute to international peace and stability, as one country is unlikely to attack another if it knows that the other country has bought a large number of weapons. Some people suggest that this leads to an 'arms race', with countries spending unwisely just to keep up with each other.

✱ STATISTICALLY SPEAKING

• From 1998 to 2001, the USA, the UK and France earned more income from arms sales to developing countries than they gave in aid.
• The five permanent members of the UN Security Council – France, Russia, China, the UK and the USA – account for 88% of the world's conventional arms exports.

YES 'From the Opium War in 1840 to the founding of the People's Republic of China in 1949, China had been bullied and humiliated by Western powers ... Historical facts have taught Chinese people that only an adequate national defence can guarantee the country's sovereignty, security, unification and territorial integrity.'
People's Daily Online, China

'The industry is a key part of our economy, contributing significantly ... to employment ... [it] supports the defence industry's high levels of technology development, and this brings benefits to other industry sectors through the application of military technology to civil products.'
Ministry of Defence, UK

In December 2004, the Japanese government eased its ban on arms exports. 'This is about ensuring security and dealing with new threats as the times change,' said Prime Minister Junichiro Koizumi (pictured). The Japan Business Federation had claimed that the arms export ban limited Japan's technological development. It described the new position as 'a great achievement'.

Developing countries' spending on military, and on education and health

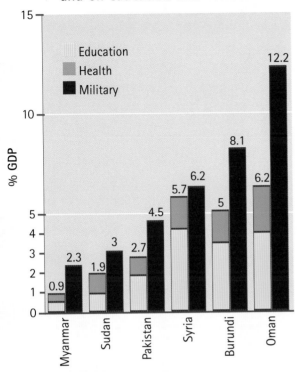

Source: Human Development Report, UNDP 2003.

'We can't have it both ways. We can't be both the world's leading champion of peace and the world's leading supplier of arms.'
Former US President Jimmy Carter

✖ 'Countries with massive development needs, such as India and South Africa, are among the UK's most [profitable] customers for military equipment. The [UK] government's support for arms sales encourages such countries to waste money – money that could be spent to meet people's basic health and education needs.'
Campaign Against the Arms Trade

✖ 'Excessive government spending on defence research and development [for the arms trade] attracts too many skilled workers away from the civil sector ... exacerbating a shortage in the non-military economy and harming prospects for long-term economic growth.'
Paul Ingram and Roy Isbister, authors

CASE STUDY

WAR AND PEACE: PREACHING WHILE SELLING ARMS

February 2002: The UK government grants 148 licences for the export of arms to India, and another 18 licenses for Pakistan.

July 2002: UK Foreign Secretary Jack Straw visits India and Pakistan to urge the leaders of these nuclear powers to pull back from the brink of war.

October 2002: UK Prime Minister Tony Blair invites Indian Prime Minister Atal Behari Vajpayee for talks on peace in Kashmir and the war on terrorism. Blair spends nearly half of his meeting asking the Indian leader to buy £1bn worth of UK built fighter jets.

Source: New Internationalist

MORE TO THINK ABOUT

Other questions to consider on the arms trade are:
Have codes of conduct to control the arms trade been effective?
Would it be possible to convert skills and machinery in the arms trade to manufacture products other than weapons?

FIND OUT MORE: www.controlarms.org www.rusi.org

Q: Should pharmaceutical patents apply in developing countries?

WHILE MOST medicines are produced in developed countries, many are needed in developing countries. New medicines can be expensive to develop, so pharmaceutical companies often put a patent – a licence – on their products. This limits others from copying it and allows companies to make their money back. However, pharmaceutical companies make most of their profits in developed countries and patents can deny people medicines who desperately need them.

YES 'Without patents, competitors who have not invested in research could easily undercut the price charged by the company that did make the investment. No company could afford to invest hundreds of millions of dollars per drug in research on such terms.'

Alan F. Holmer, Pharmaceutical Research and Manufacturers of America

'If there were better protection of product patents in India, there might be more investigation into how to deal with diseases that affect the population of that country; likewise in South Africa, Argentina and Brazil.'

Julian Morris, Director of the International Policy Network

NO 'Research and development activities would not be severely affected if patents were not extended to, and enforced in, all developing countries in the same way.'

Carlos M. Correa, University of Buenos Aires, Argentina

'I don't have the money for both my wife and I to receive antiretrovirals [the drugs that combat HIV/Aids]. If I pay for my wife, my children cannot go to school and will have no future. If I stop taking the antiretrovirals and my wife starts instead, I will die. What will happen to my family?'

John, a fisherman in Uganda

'Applying [strict] patent protection in developing countries will not generate more revenue for companies, but it will significantly limit poor people's access to vital medicines.'

Oxfam

'[Argentina, Turkey, Egypt, India and China] are the countries where we can realistically expect progress ... to implement a patent system. In giving incentives to international and domestic capitalists, they will start to produce new inventions.'

Dr Harvey Bale, International Federation of Pharmaceutical Manufacturers Associations

SOUTH AFRICA AND AIDS

The disease Aids has devastated South Africa where approximately 20% of the adult population is HIV-positive (the virus that leads to Aids). Many South Africans suffering from Aids have found that the medicines they need are too expensive.

In 2001, 39 pharmaceutical companies went to court to stop the South African government importing cheap Aids drugs. In response, some people in South Africa called on the government to declare a state of emergency over Aids, as this may have allowed the government to bypass patent laws legally and obtain cheaper drugs.

The pharmaceutical companies backed down after an international outcry over the court case, and allowed the South African government to distribute cheaper versions of patented drugs.

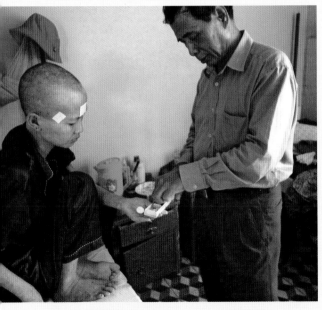

A patient receiving treatment at the Maryknoll HIV/Aids Seedling of Hope Project, Phnom Penh, Cambodia.

✪ STATISTICALLY SPEAKING

• In 2003, more than 95% of medicines on the World Health Organisation's Essential Drugs List were not patented and were generally available at low cost.

• In the developed world, under 40% of medicines are bought with personal money compared to 67% in sub-Saharan Africa and 81% in Asia and the Pacific.

• After the Brazilian government began producing generic antiretroviral drugs, prices fell 82% and Aids deaths halved.

Time lag between introduction of a new drug in the world market and its introduction in India by national firms.

Drug	Year Introduced	
	By originators in the world market	By national firms in the Indian market
Captopril	1981	1985
Ranitidine	1983	1985
Acyclovir	1985	1988
Ciprofloxacin	1985	1989

Source: B.K. Keayla

Time is crucial if generic equivalents of essential drugs are to enter into price competition before the originators secure brand loyalty.

MORE TO THINK ABOUT

Lack of essential medicines is not just a tragedy for individuals: it can have a wider impact if a country's ability to develop is hampered by high levels of sickness and by money being spent on reactive healthcare rather than on education.

Q: Should big business be allowed into schools?

BUSINESSES OFTEN provide much-needed funding for schools. This can come in the form of extra resources for the classroom, or new sports facilities, or resources for administration. Some schools welcome this answer to their budget problems and argue that, even if the business wants to advertise its products, young people are exposed to advertising all the time anyway. Others suggest that business-funded education materials may offer an incomplete point of view, and suggest that schools should be free from advertising to allow young people to develop the skills to make their own choices.

YES 'America's youth is exposed to advertising in many aspects of their lives. We believe students are savvy enough to discern between educational content and marketing materials.'

Frank Vigil, president of ZapMe!, a company that supplies US schools with free computer equipment, which features advertising

✓ 'School is ... the ideal time to influence attitudes, build long-term loyalties, introduce new products, test market, promote sampling and trial usage and – above all – to generate immediate sales.'

Lifetime Learning System advertisement

NO 'As fast-food, athletic gear and computer companies step in to fill the [funding] gap, they carry with them an educational agenda of their own. As with all branding projects, it is never enough to tag the schools with a few logos ... They are fighting for their brands to become not the add-on but the subject of education.'

Naomi Klein, author

✗ 'Our schools are being privatised not for the benefit of our children, but for the benefit of our corporations, and the export economy to which, the government hopes, they will one day contribute. Children are simply the raw materials with which they work.'

George Monbiot, author

✣ STATISTICALLY SPEAKING

• Investment banker Michael Moe estimates 10% of the $800 billion education industry will be run by for-profit corporations in 10 years time, compared to 1% today.

• The 41 million young people in the USA between ages of 5 and 14 have a direct buying power of more than $40 billion and influence $146 billion worth of expenditure every year.

• UK brands are spending an estimated £300 million a year on targeting the classroom to increase sales. Many children's food products include fundraising offers for school books, equipment or school sports clothing.

CASE STUDY 1

FOOD ADVERTISING IN SCHOOLS

US schools have been able to save money through free maths education materials from big businesses. These have come from the National Potato Board and the Snack Food Association, which produced a 'Count Your Chips' pack; from M&M's, Froot Loops and Cheerios, which have all produced counting books for young children; and from Nabisco, which had students estimate how many chocolate chips are in a bag of Chips-A-Hoy.

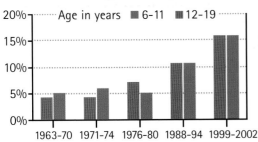

Percentage of overweight children and adolescents ages 6–19 years, USA

Age in years ▪ 6–11 ▪ 12–19

CASE STUDY 2

EDISON SCHOOLS

Edison Schools is a private company operating in schools in the USA. It is the country's largest education management organisation (EMO) with 74,000 students under its control.

To save money in schools in Philadelphia, Edison sold off textbooks, computers, lab supplies and musical instruments. It also moved company executives into schoolrooms to save $9,000 a month in rent on corporate offices.

Parents and students protest over Edison's proposed takeover of a school in New York, USA.

MORE TO THINK ABOUT

What we learn at school can have a big impact on how we see the world and our place in it. The lesson that self-worth does not depend on how many things you buy is a good place to start.

FIND OUT MORE: www.commercialexploitation.com www.edisonschools.com

Q: Do business contributions affect political decisions?

TAKING PART in elections costs political parties money. Membership of these parties is falling in many countries, so politicians have to look elsewhere for sources of income. Businesses often give donations to political parties for the publicity, and to gain contact with decision-makers. But while it is acceptable for businesses to take an active interest in policies that affect them, what if their active interest goes further and causes changes to policies that mainly benefit the business?

YES

'We must keep the lines of communication open if we want to keep passing legislation that will benefit your industry.'

From a letter written by Jim Nicholson, Chair of the US Republican Party, to Charles Heimbold Jr, CEO of Bristol-Myers Squibb

'When money has been spent to get office, the purchasers may naturally be expected to fall into the habit of trying to make a profit on the transaction.'

Aristotle, philosopher

CASE STUDY 1

THAILAND TYCOON

Thaksin Shinawatra was one of the most powerful business tycoons in Thailand in the mid-1990s, partly due to his telecoms concessions. He had to lobby to get these, and had to give rewards. In one famous instance, he gave a powerful general a Daimler car. Thaksin allegedly said to keep quiet about the gift, but the general was so proud that he drove the car to Parliament the next day, and told the first reporter who asked him about it that it came from Thaksin.

✦ STATISTICALLY SPEAKING

Do you think the present system of party funding gives too much influence over party policy to rich individuals and big business or not?

10%
16%
74%

■ Yes
■ No
■ Don't know

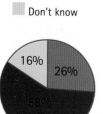

Do you think that political party funding should come mainly from taxes or do you think it should remain as it is now, with funds from party members, businesses, trade unions and wealthy individuals?

26%
16%
58%

■ Should come mainly from taxes
■ Should remain as it is now
■ Don't know

Source: ICM poll, UK

CASE STUDY 2

ROMANIAN STEEL

In 2001, UK Prime Minister Tony Blair wrote a letter backing businessman Lakshmi Mittal's bid for a Romanian steel company. Before this, Mittal paid £125,000 to Tony Blair's party. Some suggested that the Prime Minister's decision was influenced by the donation. However, others pointed out that Blair's decision was based on UK foreign policy. As early as 1989 the UK government and the European Union supported the privatisation of the Romanian steel industry, and Mittal's company had an excellent track record.

US energy company Enron paid out more than $6m in campaign contributions during the 1990s. Among those favoured were President George W Bush and his Vice-President Dick Cheney. Cheney met Enron six times while developing the US government's energy policy. Enron was declared bankrupt in 2001. Kenneth Lay (pictured), the former Chairman and CEO of Enron, was at the forefront of the political party donations.

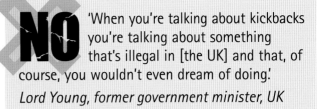

NO 'When you're talking about kickbacks you're talking about something that's illegal in [the UK] and that, of course, you wouldn't even dream of doing.'
Lord Young, former government minister, UK

✕ 'If they thought [their contributions] would buy them influence, they've blown their money.'
Spokesperson for Congressman Billy Tauzin, leader of the US House of Representatives' investigation into Enron and Arthur Andersen, and recipient of over $53,000 from the two companies since 1989

✪ STATISTICALLY SPEAKING

Transparency International survey of the sectors where the biggest bribes are likely to be paid, 2002

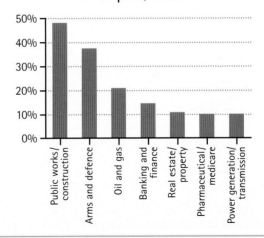

MORE TO THINK ABOUT

Why might people lose interest in the political process and faith in government if politicians give the impression that influence can be bought? Is stopping campaign contributions anti-free speech?

FIND OUT MORE: www.whitehouseforsale.org www.campaignfinance.org

Q: Are workers for big business overseas treated unfairly?

During the busy season in factories in China, some toy workers – mostly young women – work up to 15 hours a day, 7 days a week, while being paid low wages.

MOST BIG businesses are based in developed countries, yet many of their products are actually made in developing countries. Hire of factories and the cost of materials is often cheaper in these countries. Wage costs are also usually lower too. Some businesses have argued that they can bring work where otherwise there would be none. Critics say that working conditions may be dangerous, or people may be badly paid or have less freedom to form a union and campaign for better conditions.

YES 'We have to meet the quota of 1,000 pieces per day. That translates to more than a piece every minute. The quota is so high that we cannot even go to the bathroom or drink water or anything for the whole day.'
Alvaro Saavedra Anzures, Mexican worker

✓ 'Improved monitoring will not address the most difficult question facing Gap and other companies with an increasing percentage of their production in China – how to encourage respect for freedom of association in a country where that right is severely restricted by law.'
Maquila Solidarity Network

❇ STATISTICALLY SPEAKING

• Over 90% of all athletic footwear is produced in three countries: China, Indonesia and Vietnam.

Price make-up of a € 100 (£70) sports shoe

Production costs €1,50
Profit subcontractor €3
Labour costs workers €0,50
VAT €17
Material €8,50
Transport and tax €5
Publicity brand name €8
Labour costs retailer €18
Research €11
Profit brand name €13
Rent/stocks retailer €12
Publicity retailer €2,50

CONFLICTING EVIDENCE?

'The observance of human rights at all our global production sites is one of our fundamental requirements ... goals cannot and must not be realised on the grounds of exploitative activities such as child labour or forced overtime work.'

Social and environmental report, Puma

------------------- ⬇ -------------------

'My monthly wage is conditional upon completing my daily target. If I don't complete my daily target within the regular work hours I have to work overtime without pay to finish my target.'

Fatima, a worker in an Indonesian factory supplying Fila, Nike, Adidas, Puma and Lotto

NO 'US companies provide leadership in improving environmental, health and safety and energy efficiency standards through their Latin American subsidiaries. These firms export US codes of worker safety management practices and international environmental standards to Latin America.'
Business Roundtable

✖ 'Those who vent their moral indignation over low pay for Third World workers of multinational companies ignore the fact that these workers' employers usually supply them with better opportunities than they had before, while those who are morally indignant on their behalf provide them nothing.'
Thomas Sowell, journalist

✖ 'We turn to third-party garment manufacturers to produce the clothes we sell. Selecting the right manufacturers around the world – a process called sourcing – is critical to our success. We ... work to find the best factories – both in terms of product quality and commitment to treating garment workers with dignity and respect.'
GAP Inc

MORE TO THINK ABOUT

When a business bases its factories overseas, this decision impacts not just on the place that the factory goes to, but also on the place that it comes from.

How difficult do you think it is for firms to ensure that their overseas businesses are running ethically?

Q: Will big business solve climate change?

MANY SCIENTISTS HAVE said that the global climate is changing in unpredictable ways and cuts in emissions of greenhouse gases have to take place in the near future to avoid climate chaos. One of the main ways in which greenhouse gases are emitted is through the burning of fossil fuels such as oil, gas and coal. Decisions on how to solve climate change are therefore of great interest to any big business that has fossil fuels as a key resource, or as a key product.

Climate change means more unpredictable weather patterns and more intense storms.

YES '[The Business Roundtable] decided that we had to not just pay attention to what science tells us about global warming. We also have to develop cost-effective measures to reduce, avoid, sequester or offset greenhouse gas emissions.'

John J Castellani, President, Business Roundtable

'Business has the resources and focus on innovation to drive a clean energy future ... Successful companies understand what it means to lead. In this spirit, businesses have much to contribute toward dealing with climate change.'

Foreword, 'A Climate of Innovation: Northeast Business Action to Reduce Greenhouse Gases'

'By reducing greenhouse emissions and [increasing] new climate-friendly technologies, US companies can create jobs and launch an era of economic growth akin to the start-up phase of the Internet. If CEOs [Chief Executive Officers] in the United States fail to realise these opportunities, their companies will soon fall far behind overseas competitors.'

Timothy E Wirth, President, UN Foundation and Mindy S Lubber, Executive Director, Ceres

NO 'Esso ... has funded think-tanks and lobby groups to the tune of $12 million since 1997. These groups are involved both in lobbying governments directly and appearing in the media as 'independent experts' who question the reality of climate change and oppose efforts to address it.'

Greenpeace

✗ 'The environmental havoc wreaked on Tasmania [when 3,000 hectares of native forests were replaced with fast-growing eucalyptus] will earn the Japanese power company carbon credits [the right to emit greenhouse gases in exchange for planting trees] worth 130,000 metric tons of carbon dioxide emissions, allowing it to continue polluting from its Japanese power plants.'

Corporate Europe Observatory

✺ STATISTICALLY SPEAKING

• Average annual economic losses from weather-related disasters have risen from $26 billion in the 1980s to $67 billion over the last decade.

• In the 2005 Annual General Meeting season in the US, shareholders filed a record number of 31 global warming resolutions, for example on plans to reduce greenhouse gas emissions.

2004 survey of attitudes to climate change by big businesses:

• 100% think that global warming is a major or significant problem
• 93% think that climate change will increase their costs
• 85% think that climate risks will play a bigger role in 'strategic planning' in future
• 37% of companies do not consider environmental risk factors, such as extreme weather and flooding, when considering business locations

Beyond Oil?

Name of corporation	$ spent on renewables	% of total investments
BP Amoco	50 million	3
Shell	100 million	0.1
ExxonMobil	insignificant	insignificant
ChevronTexaco	275 million	2.8

MORE TO THINK ABOUT

Does overall energy use have to be re-thought in the face of climate change? What balance is needed between business action and personal action on climate change?

FIND OUT MORE: www.wbcsd.ch www.carbontradewatch.org
www.risingtide.org.uk

Q: Do citizens benefit when mergers take place?

BUSINESSES SOMETIMES join together in a process known as a merger. Their reasons for doing this vary: they may want a greater share of the market; or they may want to merge with a company from another country to establish an international presence. Regulatory bodies may pay particular attention to mergers if they think the size of the new business will give it too much say over the marketplace.

CASE STUDY

BRAND EXTENSION

Mergers do not just take place between companies selling the same products. Businesses may want to increase their brand recognition by buying enterprises that are similar but not the same. For example, when Viacom bought Blockbuster Video and Paramount Pictures in 1994, it bought the opportunity to profit from Paramount films when they were shown in cinemas and when they came out on video as well.

YES

'At a national and global level, large enterprises have the opportunity to advance public policy. In the US, this could mean helping to reshape the dysfunctional healthcare system. Worldwide, mega-companies can do much more to push for trade negotiations that have a meaningful impact on economic development.'

Financial Times

'Strength plus strength will equal success as a very strong Gillette combines with an equally strong Procter & Gamble. We will create a global company built upon scale, diversity and brand strength – all requisites for consistent growth in a consolidating, highly competitive global environment. This is an opportunity to help build something that Gillette has been pursuing for four years ... to become the best consumer products company in the world.'

James M Kilts, chairman, president and CEO of The Gillette Company

'This combination [of GlaxoWellcome buying SmithKline Beecham] will help GlaxoSmithKline to become the most productive research organisation in the pharmaceuticals industry.'

GlaxoSmithKline

NO

'Where multinationals merge with, or acquire concerns in developing countries, the result can be the creation of monopolies. If, as a result, prices in the host country are driven higher, rather than providing investment, the result of a merger can be a reverse flow of investment out of a developing country. Moreover, the size and influence of multinational corporations once located in the host country can threaten national economic sovereignty.'

New Economics Foundation

'The pharmaceutical industry now operates like a powerful drug cartel in terms of its market control, political influence and impact on the health and wealth of society.'

Julian Oram, New Economics Foundation

❖ STATISTICALLY SPEAKING

• The wave of pharmaceutical mergers in the 1990s, worth a combined $200 billion, led to the loss of around 100,000 jobs – about 20% of the industry's total workforce.

• Of the 100 largest announcements of mergers upto 2002, 84 occurred during the years 1996 to 2000.

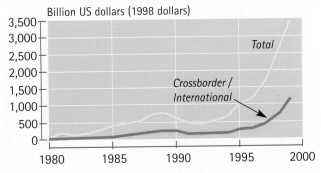

Worldwide mergers and acquisitions 1980 – 1999

Billion US dollars (1998 dollars)

Total

Crossborder / International

Source: Thomson Financial Securities Data

'If the whole idea of this revolution is to empower people, Bill [Bill Gates, pictured] why are you locking up the market and restricting choices? Synergising your way from one [business] to another every month?'

Email to Bill Gates of Microsoft from Andrew Shapiro, a fellow at Harvard Law School

MORE TO THINK ABOUT

There are issues around the broader impact of mergers on society. For example, mergers in the media industry may lead to less diversity of opinion in the media, or mergers in the pharmaceutical industry may limit people's access to affordable drugs.

Q: is big always best?

High streets in cities around the world are increasingly full of the same shops and restaurants that sell the same products wherever they are. Some people have suggested that this brings more goods to more people. Others have said that the possibility of finding unique and varied products fades a bit more each time a local business is replaced by a national or global chain.

Big BUSINESSES usually seem set on getting even bigger through buying or merging with another company, or through selling more products. Getting bigger may mean bigger profits and more influence in a particular market. On the other hand, it may mean that the business is stretched so thinly that it is difficult to manage. Some businesses have also been criticised for being so big that they invest their profits far away from the place where goods are produced or sold.

YES

'I can't begin to count the number of times that people who run consumer businesses have confided to me that their goal is to create the broad-based success that Disney seems to bring to every project and every business it touches.'

Michael J Wolf, management consultant

'Thanks to their deep financial resources, big companies can attract and retain employees with benefits that most small companies just aren't in a position to offer.'

H Michael Boyd, human resourcing strategies program manager

'It may be right that Mars sticks to the chocolate bar and Nike keeps its feet on the ground. But if their executives cross the Atlantic on a Virgin plane, listen to Virgin records and keep their money with a Virgin bank, then at least Britain will have one new global brand for the next century.'

Richard Branson, businessman

NO

'I realised that there was only one way to go: with a small firm that would recognise my individual needs and give me the chance to prove my potential.'

Patrick McGinness, graduate,
University of Maryland, USA

✖ 'It [may be] possible to fulfill a society's material requirements by means of less expensive and simpler equipment than the costly, computerised, labour-saving machinery necessary for satisfying the massive appetite for ... commodities.'

Leopold Kohr, Schumacher UK

✖ '"Bigness" [tends to squeeze out of the corporation] the human understanding, the human sympathy, the human contacts, and the natural human relationships.'

AT & T telecoms business, vice president

CASE STUDY

DAVID AND GOLIATH OF THE COMPUTER WORLD

Microsoft dominates the world of computer software. Its Windows operating system is used on 95% of computers in the world. It is so big that Jonathan Schwartz of a rival company has suggested that: 'The threat that Microsoft poses is to turn the Internet into a company town – Microsoft town.'

Microsoft's dominance of the software market is being challenged by the Linux system. This works in a very different way to the Microsoft system. Unlike the Windows giant, which largely keeps information on its software to itself, information on Linux is available for free from the Internet and can be updated by any of its users.

✿ STATISTICALLY SPEAKING

• Seven media corporations run the major US film studios, control 80–85% of the global music market, dominate worldwide satellite broadcasting, control a significant percentage of book publishing and commercial magazine publishing, own all or part of most commercial cable TV channels worldwide and operate a large amount of European terrestrial television.

Food is big business. The UK has become largely dependent on food grown overseas, distributed through supermarkets.

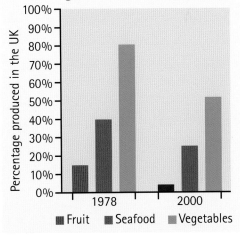

UK self-sufficiency in fruit, vegetables and seafood

MORE TO THINK ABOUT

The strength of big businesses used to come from economies of scale, where the average cost of a product was reduced when the volume of production increased. Nowadays a business's ability to manage itself as a global brand is also very important.

Q: Can economic globalisation end poverty?

IN THE past, the economies of countries were run in different ways. From about 1980, governments started to organise their economies in the same way, removing barriers to trade and investment and selling off state-owned industries. This allowed companies that operated in several nations to flourish. The era of economic globalisation had begun.

CASE STUDY

HAITI RICE

The Caribbean island of Haiti wanted money from the World Bank and the International Monetary Fund (IMF).

In return, the World Bank and the IMF demanded an end to tax on foreign rice. The result was that Haiti was flooded with American rice that could be sold more cheaply because the US government was giving its rice farmers billions of dollars a year and they had better equipment. As a result, Haitian rice farmers struggled to make a living.

YES 'If the poorest countries can be drawn into the global economy and get increasing access to modern knowledge and technology, it could lead to a rapid reduction in global poverty – as well as bringing new trade and investment opportunities for all.'
Tony Blair, Prime Minister, UK

'Globalisation leads to economic growth and higher incomes. No country has benefited for any length of time from closed-door policies, and the countries that have achieved most prosperity have embraced globalisation, together with the policies that make it work.'
The International Monetary Fund

✪ STATISTICALLY SPEAKING

• World Bank economists David Dollar and Aart Kraay analysed data from 125 countries, gathered over 40 years. They found that incomes rise as growth takes place and that, on average, the income levels of the poorest fifth of the population rise at the same rate as the overall rate. They concluded that 'globalisation is good for the poor'.

NO

'Wage inequality has increased in almost all developing countries that have undertaken rapid trade liberalisation [the removal of barriers to trade and investment] ... By the beginning of 1999, there were some 150 million people unemployed worldwide and up to one billion under-employed – a third of the world's labour force.'

Michael Woodin and Caroline Lucas, authors of 'Green Alternatives to Globalisation'

✗ 'Globalisation is putting the clock back as it reduces the security, basic needs provision and employment prospects for billions for whom things had been improving since the Second World War.'

Colin Hines, economist and author

✿ STATISTICALLY SPEAKING

• Some 54 countries are poorer now than in 1990. A larger proportion of people are going hungry in 21 countries. In 14 countries, more children are dying before the age of five. In 12 countries, primary school enrolments are shrinking. Life expectancy has fallen in 34 countries.

Human Development Report, 2003

MORE TO THINK ABOUT

The argument over whether economic globalisation helps the poor doesn't just hang on whether they now have more money. Critics argue that communities can fall apart if the rich have a great deal more than the poor and that having more money may be at the cost of hardships such as having to leave your family to find work.

A Coca-Cola billboard next to a stand pipe in Sierra Leone's capital. Many houses in the capital still don't have running water.

FIND OUT MORE: www.undp.org www.wto.org www.twnside.org.sg

Glossary

Asset property owned by a person or company.

Bankrupt legally declared unable to pay your debts.

Barriers to trade restrictions on trade; sometimes involves a cost that increases the price of the traded product.

Brand a type of product manufactured by a company under a particular name.

Brand loyalty repeated buying of a product or service.

Brand recognition wide knowledge of a name, logo or image associated with a product or service.

Bureaucracy the administration – such as office or management systems – of an organisation.

Business roundtable a grouping of business representatives.

Cabinet Secretary (US) the head of a government department in the US.

Capital wealth that is owned, invested, lent, or borrowed.

Capitalism an economic system run as described in 'capitalist economy'.

Capitalist economy an economic system where assets are controlled by private owners for profit.

Carbon credits units used to account for, and trade in, carbon dioxide emissions.

Carbon dioxide an atmospheric gas made up of carbon and oxygen; one of the main greenhouse gases.

CEO, Chief Executive Officer the person responsible for seeing that plans and policies set by a business's board of directors are carried out.

Corporate Social Responsibility the awareness, acceptance and management of the implications and effects of decisions made by big businesses.

Developed country a higher income country.

Developing country a lower income country.

Dictatorship a country governed by a ruler with total power.

Economic growth the increase in the value of goods and services produced by an economy.

Economic sovereignty having full control over economic affairs.

Economist an expert in economics.

Fossil fuel a fuel such as oil, coal or gas, formed over many, many years from the remains (fossils) of living organisms.

Free agency the position of a professional athlete who is free to negotiate a contract to play for any team.

Freedom of association the right to form societies, clubs, and other groups of people, and to meet with people without interference by the government.

Free trade in theory this is trade that takes place without restrictions such as trade barriers. In practice, free trade agreements sometimes actually impose trade restrictions.

FTSE 100 the Financial Times Stock Exchange Index of 100 Leading Shares is a report on the shares of the 100 largest companies listed on the London Stock Exchange. Also used to refer to these 100 largest companies as a group.

Generic [drug] a drug identical to a brand name drug but usually sold at a lower price.

Grass-root level at the level of ordinary citizens, as opposed to larger organisations or wealthy individuals.

Greenhouse gases gases in the Earth's atmosphere that absorb solar radiation and act like a greenhouse by trapping in heat. Greenhouse gases include water vapour, carbon dioxide, methane and ozone.

Infrastructure (transport) the basic physical and organisational structures that transport systems need in order to operate.

International Chamber of Commerce a global organisation made up of business representatives.

Kickbacks illegal payments made to someone who has helped with a deal or a trade arrangement.

Legislation a set of laws for a country.

Lobby to try to influence someone, for example, a politician.

Lobbyist someone who is paid to lobby decision-makers.

Merger the process of combining more than one company.

Non–Governmental Organisation (NGO) an organisation that is independent from the government. Usually, but not always, refers to non-commercial groups.

Offset to balance out or compensate for something.

OPEC the Organisation of the Petroleum Exporting Countries, which co-ordinates petroleum policies among oil-producing countries.

Opium War one of two wars that took place in the 19th Century between China and Western countries over British drug-trafficking.

Patent a government licence giving an individual or organisation the right to make, use, or sell an invention.

Pesticide a substance for destroying insects or unwanted wildlife.

Privatisation the transfer of ownership from government-owned to a privately-owned business.

Requisite a thing that needs to be done to reach a particular end.

Risk-management the process of measuring risk and then developing plans to manage it.

Sequester to hold, or take possession of something.

Shareholder a person, company, or other institution that owns a part of a company. May also be called a stockholder.

Shareholder resolutions an official statement by shareholders that comments on, or requests action from, the board of directors of a business.

State of Emergency a government declaration that may suspend normal functions of government.

Stock market a place where stocks or shares are bought and sold.

Sub-contracting giving some of the work from a contract to another party.

Subsidiary a company that is controlled by another 'parent' company.

Sustainable able to meet needs and keep going over a period of time, while avoiding a serious drain on resources.

Synergising combining more than one company together.

Telecoms concession a right granted by government to operate a telecommunications business.

Think-tank a group that carries out research and develops ideas.

Union an association formed by people with a common interest or purpose.

Usury lending money at extremely high rates of interest.

Debating tips

WHAT IS DEBATING?

A debate is a structured argument. Two teams speak in turn for or against a particular question. Usually each person is given a time they are allowed to speak for and any remarks from the other side are controlled. The subject of the debate is often already decided so you may find yourself having to support opinions with which you do not normally agree. You may also have to argue as part of a team, being careful not to contradict what others on your side have said.

After both sides have had their say, and had a chance to answer the opposition, the audience votes for the side they agree with.

DEBATING SKILLS

1 Know your subject

Research it as much as you can. The debates in this book give opinions as a starting point, but there are website suggestions for you to find out more. Use facts and information to support your points.

2 Make notes

Write down key words and phrases on cards. Try not to read a prepared speech. You might end up losing your way and stuttering.

3 Watch the time

You may be given a set amount of time for your presentation, so stick to it.

4 Practise how you sound

Try to sound natural. Think about:
Speed – Speak clearly and steadily. Try to talk at a pace that is fast enough to sound intelligent and allows you time to say what you want, but slow enough to be understood.
Tone – Varying the tone of your voice will make you sound interesting.
Volume – Speak at a level at which everyone in the room can comfortably hear you. Shouting does not win debates. Variation of volume (particularly speaking more quietly at certain points) can help you to emphasise important points but the audience must still be able to hear you.
Don't ramble – Short, clear sentences work well and are easier to understand.

GET INVOLVED - NATIONAL DEBATING LEAGUES

Worldwide links
www.debating.net

Debating Matters, UK
www.debatingmatters.com

Auckland Debating Society, New Zealand
www.ada.org.nz/schlevels.php

Debaters Association of Victoria, Australia
www.debating.netspace.net.au

Index

Acknowledgements

Picture credits: © Kapoor Baldev/Sygma/Corbis: 14. © Denis Balibouse/Reuters/Corbis: 7. Digital Vision: 17, 36, 37. Franklin Watts: 35, 42. Chris Fairclough/Franklin Watts: 18, 19, 23, 30, 40. © Mark Henley/Panos Pictures: cover, 34. © Clive Shirley/Panos Pictures: 43. BYB/Rex Features: 20. Nils Jorgensen/Rex Features: 10. Ron Sachs/Rex Features: 33. Alex Segre/Rex Features: 24-25. Sipa Press/Rex Features: 4-5, 16, 26, 29.TopFoto/ImageWorks: 12, 31, 39. TopFoto/National: 8.

Text credits: Page 6: 1 Johan Olsson, 'The Power of Business In Australia-Lindblom's Theory': http://www.geocities.com/TimesSquare/1848/power.html; 2 Hank McKinnell, Speech at the launch of the Business Roundtable's Institute for Corporate Ethics, 14/1/04; 3 John J Castellani, Speech to the Singapore Technologies International Advisory Board Meeting on 'Shaping Public Policy Amid a Changing Political Landscape', 5/10/04; 4 Rebecca Spencer, p14, *Corporate Law and Structures,* http://www.corporatewatch.org.uk/publications/corporate_structures.pdf; Page 8: 1 Keith Ince 'Australia's corporate salaries soar as wages are depressed', World Socialist Web Site, 20/11/99: http://www.wsws.org/articles/1999/nov1999/wage-n20.shtml; 2 'In sickness and in wealth', *Management Today*, 1/3/04, 3 Rhymer Rigby, 'Britain's Most Overpaid Jobs', *Management Today*, 1/4/04; Page 9: 1 Jan Luthman, 'The best of the FTSE bosses', *Investors Chronicle*, 22/12/04; 2 American Federation of Labor and Congress of Industrial Organisations, Executive Paywatch, http://www.aflcio.org/corporateamerica/paywatch/; 3 George Monbiot, 'The Billion-Dollar Bonus, 18/5/00, http://www.monbiot.com/archives/2000/05/18/the-billion-dollar-bonus/. Page 10: 1 Peter Montagon, 'Shareholders taste blood as fat cat cream turns sour', *Management Issues*, 20/5/03; 2 'Use your shareholder power to help free Burma': http://www.shareholderpower.com/index.html#10/10/00; Page 11: 1 Ken Colvert quoted in 'Investors give Vodafone board a bumpy ride', *The Guardian*, 28/7/04; 2 Interview with Simon Billenness, quoted on p148, *The Corporation*, Joel Bakan, Constable, 2004; Page 12: 1 Videotaped message for the Secretary General of the United Nations, Kofi Annan, to the ICC regional conference in Abuja, 20/11/00: http://www.iccwbo.org/home/news_archives/2000/annan_speech.asp; 2 'Citizenship', http://www2.coca-cola.com/citizenship/index.html; Page 13: 1 Ken Saro Wiwa, Speech to the General Assembly of the Unrepresented Nations and Peoples Organisation, UNPO 3rd general assembly daily press release, 21/1/93: http://nativenet.uthscsa.edu/archive/nl/9301/0128.html; 2 Rebecca Spencer, p17, 'Corporate law and structures - exposing the roots of the problem': http://www.corporatewatch.org.uk/publications/corporate_structures.pdf; 3 George Soros quoted in 'Fund Management Guru Reveals Doubts', *Financial Times*, 8/12/98; Page 14: 1 Deborah Doane, Chair, CORE Coalition; 2 Benedict Southworth: http://web.amnesty.org/library/Index/ENGASA201072004?open&of=ENG-IND; Page 15: 1 Confederation of British Industry, 'Global Social Responsibility Is the business of business just business?'; 2 'First award for responsible capitalism 2004 Acceptance speech by Morris Tabaksblat KBE': http://www.reed-elsevier.com/media/pdf/p/1/SpeechFirstAward.pdf; 3 'Cape caves in on South African asbestos case', ACTSA, 13/3/03: http://www.actsa.org/News/press_releases/130303_cape.htm; 4 Richard Meeran: http://www.leighday.co.uk/doc.asp?doc=108&cat=850; Page 16: 1 Adrian Nastase, 'Private Interests: The privatisation of Romania's oil industry has enriched the well-connected and corrupt', Center for Public Integrity, 21/2/05: http://www.publicintegrity.org/oil/report.aspx?aid=598&sid=100; 2 'Colonialism and the Baku-Tbilisi-Ceyhan pipeline': http://www.bakuceyhan.org.uk/more_info/colonialism.htm; 3 Andrew Simms, P3, 'Degrees of Capture: universities, the oil industry and climate change': http://www.neweconomics.org/gen/uploads/Degrees%20of%20Capture(1).pdf; Page 17: 1 'Does OPEC control the oil market?': http://www.opec.org/library/FAQs/aboutOPEC/q13.htm; 2 Matthew Yeomans, p92, *Oil Anatomy of an Industry*, The New Press 2004; 3 Lord Browne, Major Projects Association Prestige Lecture,

9/6/04: http://www.bp.com/genericarticle.do?categoryId=98&contentId=2018753; Page 18: 1 Tony Hague: http://news.bbc.co.uk/1/hi/talking_point/864514.stm; 2 Greg Palast, 'A Tale of Two Coups: Venezuela and Argentina', 3/7/02: http://www.corpwatch.org/article.php?id=2908; 3 Muhammad Yunus, 'Grameen Bank': http://www.grameen-info.org/bank/index.html; Page 19: 1 'Getting real banking choice', editorial *Sydney Morning Herald* , 21 May 2005; 2 Horia Paraschivescu: http://news.bbc.co.uk/1/hi/talking_point/864514.stm; Page 20: 1 'Overview: Athens hopes for defining moment in the sun', *Financial Times*, 31/8/04; 2 Tedy Brushci, 'Much more than money', SI.com in Yahoo Sports, 8/2/05; 3 Ashish S. Chavan quoted in 'Has commercialisation helped sports?', Dignity Foundation: http://www.dignityfoundation.com/october2004sports.html; 4 Tim Crow quoted in 'Business relations: When Beckham hits the target, companies hope to gain', *Financial Times*, 23/8/04; Page 22: 1 Quoted in 'Strange fruit', fruitnet.com, 9/9/02, http://www.fruitnet.com/cgi-bin/features.pl?features.REF=35; 2 Lucy Michaels, p15, 'What's wrong with supermarkets', http://www.corporatewatch.org.uk/publications/agriculture/www_sm_v4.pdf; 3 Kosol Somchinda quoted in 'Superstore: Call for freeze on superstores', Siam Future, 30/4/02: http://www.siamfuture.com/thainews/thnewstxt.asp?tid=1244; Page 25: 1 Fiona Moriarty quoted in 'Scotland – Green Party wrong on supermarket claims', British Retail Consortium, 24/11/04: http://www.brc.org.uk/details04.asp?id=496&kCat=&kData=1; 2 *Daily Mail* article quoted in 'Economic Cleansing', Monbiot.com, 17/6/99: http://www.monbiot.com/archives/1999/06/17/economic-cleansing/; Page 26: 1 'Editorial: China's Defence Policy Equals Peace', 10/3/00: http://english1.people.com.cn/english/200003/10/eng20000310O101.html; 2 Foreword, Defence Industrial Policy, October 2002: http://www.mod.uk/issues/industrial_policy/foreword.htm; Page 27: 1 Jimmy Carter, Presidential campaign, 1976, http://www.controlarms.org/the_issues/arms_industry.htm; 2 'The arms trade: An Introductory Briefing', September 2001, http://www.caat.org.uk/information/publications/other/intro-briefing-0901.php; 3 Paul Ingram and Roy Isbister, p5, 'Escaping the subsidy trap: why arms exports are bad for Britain', British American Security Information Council, Saferworld and Oxford Research Group: http://www.oxfordresearchgroup.org.uk/publications/books/ORGsubsidy.pdf; Page 28: 1 Alan F Holmer, 'The Case for Innovation: The Role of Intellectual Property Protection', The Economist's Second Annual Pharmaceuticals Roundtable, 20/11/02, http://www.phrma.org/publications/publications/20.11.2002.629.cfm; 2 Julian Morris, quoted in 'Owning knowledge', 'Bringing Treatments, Developing Cures', *The Pfizer Journal*, http://www.thepfizerjournal.com/default.asp?a=article&tj=tpj30&tt=Bringing%20Treatments%2C%20Developing%20Cures; 3 Dr Harvey Bale, p32, 'The Realities of Patent Protection Around the World', *The Pfizer Journal*, Global Edition Volume 1, Number 2, 2000; 4 Carlos M Correa quoted in 'Bringing Treatments, Developing Cures', *The Pfizer Journal*; 5 p4, 'US bullying on drug patents: one year after Doha', Oxfam: http://www.oxfam.org.uk/what_we_do/issues/health/downloads/bp33_bullying.pdf; 6 'Implausible Denial; Why the Drug Giants' Arguments on Patents Don't Stack Up', Oxfam, April 2001 quoted in 'Patents, pills and public health: Can TRIPS deliver?, The Panos Institute 2002: http://www.panos.org.uk/PDF/reports/TRIPS_low_res.pdf; Page 30: 1 Frank Vigil quoted in 'ZapMe! Invites Ralph Nader back to school', PR Newswire, 10/12/98, quoted on p102, *No Logo*, Naomi Klein, Flamingo, 2000; 2 Lifetime Learning System quoted in 'Captive kids: a report on commercial pressures on kids at school', 1998: http://www.consumersunion.org/other/captivekids/pressures.htm; 3 Naomi Klein, p89 *No Logo*, Flamingo, 2000; Page 32: 1 Jim Nicholson quoted in 'Documents show parties often mix fund-raising and policy', *The New York Times*, 7/12/02, quoted on p105, *The Corporation*, Joel Bakan, Constable, 2004; 2 Aristotle; Page 33: 1 Lord Young, Reference 18 in *Exporting Corruption*, The Corner House, June 2000: http://www.thecornerhouse.org.uk/item.shtml?x=51975#fn018 (speaking on BBC Radio 4, 'Talking Politics' in 1994, quoted from official transcript of 'Bribes', transmitted by

BBC Radio 4 on 28/496); 2 Spokesperson for Congressman Billy Tauzin from: http://www.alternet.org/columnists/story/12296/; Page 34: 1 Alvaro Saavedra Anzures quoted in 'Frequently Asked Questions: 'Free Trade' and Sweatshops', Global Exchange, 22/7/04: http://www.globalexchange.org/campaigns/sweatshops/sweatshopsfaq.html; 2 'Gap CSR report raises transparency bar', 'Codes Memo: Number 17', July 2004, Maquila Solidarity Network: http://www.maquilasolidarity.org/resources/codes/memo17.htm; Page 35: 1 Quoted on p112, 'Sportswear Industry Data and Company Profiles: Background information for the Play Fair at the Olympics Campaign', Clean Clothes Campaign, 1/3/04: http://www.cleanclothes.org/ftp/Background%20Company%20Profiles%20Olympics%20Campaign.pdf; 2 Quoted on p122, Sportswear Industry Data and Company Profiles: Background information for the Play Fair at the Olympics Campaign', Clean Clothes Campaign, 1/3/04: http://www.cleanclothes.org/ftp/Background%20Profiles%20Olympics%20Campaign.pdf; 3 'Beyond the Balance Sheet: How US companies bring positive change to Latin America', Business Roundtable, 2/4/04, http://www.businessroundtable.org/pdf/595.pdf; 4 Thomas Sowell, 'Sweatshops Part II', Washington Times, 31/1/04, http://www.washtimes.com/commentary/20040131-104831-7264r.htm; 5 'How our clothes are made', Gap Inc: http://www.gapinc.com/social_resp/ifpr/how_made.htm; Page 36: 1 John J Castellani, 'Speech to the Singapore Technologies International Advisory Board Meeting on 'Shaping Public Policy Amid a Changing Political Landscape', 5/10/04: http://www.businessroundtable.org/newsroom/document.aspx?qs=5936BF807822B0F1AD44E8322FB51711FCF53CE; 2 'A Climate of Innovation: Northeast Business Action to Reduce Greenhouse Gases', World Resources Institute 2004: http://pdf.wri.org/cne_foreward.pdf; 3 Timothy E Wirth, 'US companies face challenges as Europe and other countries move to limit greenhouse emissions', *Boston Globe*, 30/12/04: http://www.ceres.org/newsroom/press/lubber_oped_123004.htm; Page 37: 1 'The case against Esso', Greenpeace, http://www.greenpeace.org/climate/climatecriminals/esso/case.cfm; 2 'High Time for UN to Break 'Partnership' with the ICC', Corporate Europe Observatory, 25/7/01, http://www.corporateeurope.org/un/icc.html; Page 38: 1 'Why Goliaths need to be careful', *Financial Times*, 28/2/05, http://news.ft.com/cms/s/325913fc-892d-11d9-b7ed-00000e2511c8.html; 2 James M. Kilts, 'Gillette CEO Views Combination with P&G as Leading to New Era of Growth', Business Wire, 24/2/05, http://phx.corporate-ir.net/phoenix.zhtml?c=106746&p=irol-newsArticleProduct&t=Regular&id=678678&; Page 39: 1 p8, mergerwatch edition 1, 9/4/01, New Economics Foundation: http://www.neweconomics.org/gen/uploads/doc_104200142311_mergerwatchone.pdf; 2 Julian Oram, New Economics Foundation, 'Addicted to Profit', Corporate Breakdown Edition 2/9/02, http://www.neweconomics.org/gen/uploads/gx2dcv45szxpsn55yohg3rjh01082003160233.pdf; 3 Andrew Shapiro, 'Memo to Chairman Bill', Nation, 10/11/97, quoted on p164 *No Logo*, Naomi Klein, Flamingo, 2000; Page 40: 1 Michael J Wolf p224, 'The Entertainment Economy', quoted on p146, *No Logo*, Flamingo 2000; 2 'Size Counts', Graduating Engineer Online, http://www.graduatingengineer.com/articles/feature/08-08-00b.html; 3 Richard Branson quoted on p148, *No Logo*, Naomi Klein, Flamingo, 2000; Page 41: 1 Patrick McGinness quoted in 'Size Counts', Graduating Engineer Online, http://www.graduatingengineer.com/articles/feature/08-08-00b.html; 2 Leopold Kohr, 'About E F Schumacher', Schumacher UK: http://www.schumacher.org.uk/about_efschumacher.htm; 2 AT & T vice-president quoted on p17, 'The Corporation', Joel Bakan, Constable 2004; Page 42: 1 Tony Blair in 'Eliminating World Poverty: Making Globalisation Work for the Poor', White Paper on International Development, December 2000; 2 IMF Staff, 'Debt Relief, Globalisation, and IMF Reform: Some Questions and Answers': http://www.imf.org/external/np/exr/ib/2000/041200b.htm, 12/4/00; Page 43: 1 Michael Woodin, Caroline Lucas, *Green Alternatives to Globalisation: A Manifesto*, Pluto Press Ltd, 2004; 2 Colin Hines, 'Time to Replace Globalisation with Localisation', *Global Environmental Politics*, Volume 3, Number 3, August 2003